# Making a Little Raft

Debbie Croft

Photographs by Lindsay Edwards

## Contents

Goal                2

Materials           2

Steps               4

Glossary            16

# Goal

To make a little **raft**.

# Materials

You will need:

- 7 big sticks
- 2 little sticks
- red card

- 5 yellow stars
- string
- play dough
- scissors
- a pencil
- a tub of water.

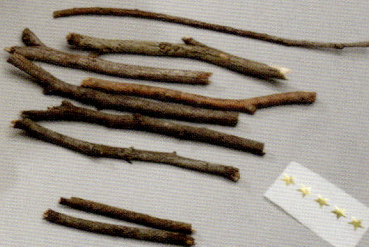

# Steps

**1.** Six big sticks go here to make the raft.

**2.** The little sticks go on the big sticks like this.

**3.** Cut some string with the scissors.

**4.** Make the string go over and under the sticks like this.

**5.** Make a ball

with the play dough.

**6.** The ball of play dough goes here on the raft.

**7.** Draw a **sail**

on the red card.

Cut it out.

**8.** The five yellow stars go on the sail.

**9.** Get Mum

to cut two holes

in the sail.

The biggest stick
goes into the holes
to make the mast.

**10.** The mast goes into the play dough on the raft.

**11.** The raft can go on the water.

# Glossary

raft

sail